Endangered ANIMALS

Jan Sovak

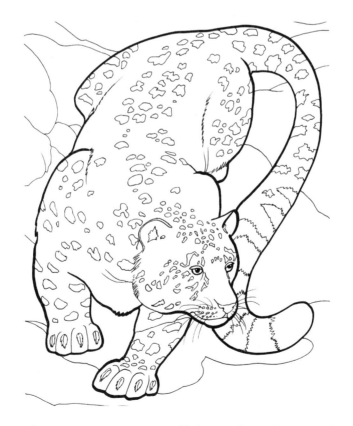

DOVER PUBLICATIONS, INC.
Mineola, New York

NOTE

There are so many reasons why a species could be threatened with extinction. When an animal is extinct, it no longer exists on earth. Global warming, disease and viruses, loss of habitat to human population, oil spills, drought, hunters, and accidents are just some of the causes that contribute to an animal becoming endangered.

Animals at risk of becoming extinct are assessed by the IUCN (International Union for Conservation of Nature). It is then determined which of the seven categories the animals will fall under: extinct, extinct in the wild, critical, endangered, vulnerable, near threatened, and least concern. Every effort is made to help these animals, including captive breeding programs, relocation to a protected area, and conservation actions to protect their habitats. As their numbers improve or decline, they are moved into a different category—it's always changing from year to year!

Thanks to the government, conservation programs, non-profit groups, and community organizations, these animals might have a second chance and be able to thrive in their natural surroundings.

Copyright

Copyright © 2009 by Dover Publications, Inc.
All rights reserved.

Bibliographical Note

Endangered Animals is a new work, first published by Dover Publications, Inc., in 2009.

DOVER *Pictorial Archive* SERIES

This book belongs to the Dover Pictorial Archive Series. You may use the designs and illustrations for graphics and crafts applications, free and without special permission, provided that you include no more than four in the same publication or project. (For permission for additional use, please write to Permissions Department, Dover Publications, Inc., 31 East 2nd Street, Mineola, N.Y. 11501.)

However, republication or reproduction of any illustration by any other graphic service, whether it be in a book or in any other design resource, is strictly prohibited.

International Standard Book Number
ISBN-13: 978-0-486-46793-1
ISBN-10: 0-486-46793-7

Manufactured in the United States of America
Dover Publications, Inc., 31 East 2nd Street, Mineola, N.Y. 11501

evy's Zebra *(Equus grevyi)*. They are the larg-
of all zebras, weighing as much as 950 pounds
standing close to five-feet tall. They eat grass
and leaves, and can survive for many days without food and water. These zebras are native to
Kenya and Ethiopia.

Red Wolf (*Canis lupus rufus*). These meat eaters are medium-sized members of the canine family and ancestors of the domestic dog. When full grown they weigh between forty-five and eig[ht] pounds. They can be found in the southe[rn] United States.

g Cobra *(Ophiophagus hannah)*. These poi-
ous snakes can reach up to eighteen feet in
gth and can stand high enough to look a
son in the eye. This snake's venom can kill
an elephant in one bite! King Cobras live in the
rainforests and plains of Southeast Asia, India,
and southern China.

Whooping Crane *(Grus americana)*. These beautiful cranes are the tallest flying birds in North America. They have a wingspan of seven to eight feet and can weigh up to seventeen pounds. They only be found in protected nesting locations Canada and the United States.

4

alrus *(Odobenus rosmarus)*. They are the larg- animals with four flippers in the Arctic and barctic. The tusks of a male walrus can grow to four-feet long; female tusks are two-feet long. Walruses can weigh anywhere between one and two tons. They are bottom feeders and spend two-thirds of their life in the water.

Arabian Oryx *(Oryx leucoryx)*. These medium-sized antelopes became extinct in the wild, but after a captive breeding conservation program they have been reintroduced into protected are of Saudi Arabia. They can walk long distan and can survive for weeks without water.

Black-footed Ferret (*Mustela nigripes*). Originally found in North America, these weasel-like creatures spend ninety percent of their time underground. They hunt at night and their diet consists of mostly prairie dogs—their favorite food! These ferrets can eat up to 100 prairie dogs a year!

Three-toed Sloth (*Bradypus tridactylus*). These slow-moving mammals live in the rainforest canopies of Central and South America. They sleep, eat, mate, and even give birth hanging upside-down in trees. Their diet consists of fr leaves, small twigs, and buds. Their only form protection is to blend in with the rainforest.

Humpback Whale *(Megaptera novaeangliae).* These marine mammals are found worldwide and migrate from polar waters in the summer to tropical and subtropical waters in the winter. They measure forty- to fifty-feet long and weigh between twenty-five and forty tons. Humpbacks are known for their jumping and rolling around.

Indian Rhinoceros *(Rhinoceros unicornis).* These rhinos have one horn and skin folds that make them look like they are wearing a coat of armor. They weigh up to 4,400 pounds and can live for years or more. Indian rhinos are native to northern India and Nepal.

10

een Turtle *(Chelonia mydas).* These sea turtles e found mainly in tropical and subtropical ters and in the Atlantic and Pacific oceans. They grow as large as five-feet long and can weigh up to 440 pounds. They are one of the few species that have been around since the dinosaurs.

Ivory-billed Woodpecker (*Campephilus principalis*). These are the largest woodpeckers in North America and the second largest in the world. Thought to be extinct, there was a sighting in Arkansas in 2005. That was the last time th were spotted. The search continues to this d for this rare bird.

12

guar (*Panthera onca*). They are the largest cats the Americas, weighing 100 to 250 pounds at aturity. They can be found in parts of the southwest United States and most of Mexico and South America. These meat eaters have great vision and hunt at night.

Giant Panda (*Ailuropoda melanoleuca*). These black-and-white bears are native to the bamboo forests in the mountain ranges of central China. Their diet consists mainly of bamboo. They can consume up to forty pounds of bamboo per d[...] These pandas can weigh as much as 250 poun[...] A new baby panda weighs only four ounces.

Gorilla (*Gorilla gorilla*). These "gentle giants" are the largest of all primates. They live in the forests of western Africa. They are plant eaters and consume approximately forty pounds of food per day. Gorillas can weigh up to 500 pounds and can live thirty-five years in the wild. A gorilla's nose is like a human fingerprint—no two are alike!

Kakapo *(Strigops habroptilus)*. Also known as the owl parrot, these birds are the only parrots that are nocturnal and cannot fly. Their only defense is to stand still. They are also the heaviest parrots—weighing up to nine pounds! They a the rarest parrots in the world and are native New Zealand.

Giant Armadillo (*Priodontes maximus*). They are the largest species of armadillos and weigh between forty and seventy pounds. Their favorite food is termites. These creatures are native to South America, mostly within the Amazon basin. Armadillos come out at night and are excellent diggers.

Komodo Dragon *(Varanus komodoensis)*. These reptiles are the largest living lizards on earth, averaging eight-feet long and weighing 200 pounds. They are native to four southeastern Indonesian islands in the Lesser Sundra regic They will eat just about anything and can eighty percent of their body weight in one me

18

Chimpanzee *(Pan troglodytes)*. These primates live in the tropical forests by the equator in Africa. They are the closest living relatives to humans. They are one of the few animals that can make "tools" in order to eat and drink. Chimps can live up to forty years in the wild.

Manatee (*Trichechus manatus*). These gentle, slow-moving marine mammals are also known as sea cows. They are plant eaters and can consume ten percent of their body weight in one day. They a native to North and South Atlantic waters, t coast of Mexico, the Caribbean, and the Amaz

rangutan (*Pongo pygmaeus*). These apes spend ost of their time in trees. Orangutans are the orld's most intelligent animals next to humans. ney live in the rainforests on the islands of Borneo and Sumatra. Their shaggy reddish-brown hair makes them easy to recognize. They stand almost six-feet tall and can weigh 260 pounds.

Cheetah *(Acinonyx jubatus)*. These cats are the fastest land animals; running as fast as seventy-five miles per hour. They are meat eaters and use their sight, not smell, to locate prey. Cheetahs a located in Africa, south of the Sahara Desert.

ild Yak *(Bos grunniens)*. They are excellent mbers and live in the highest altitude of any ammal (over 19,000 feet). Yaks can survive in temperatures as low as forty below zero. Their dense, wooly coat acts as insulation in extreme temperatures. They are native to Tibet.

Sea Otter *(Enhydra lutris)*. They are the largest members of the weasel family, weighing up to 100 pounds. These carnivores are one of the few animals to use "tools." They have the thickest fur of all animals (250,000 hairs per square inch). Sea otters can be found from California, Alaska, Russia, and Japan.

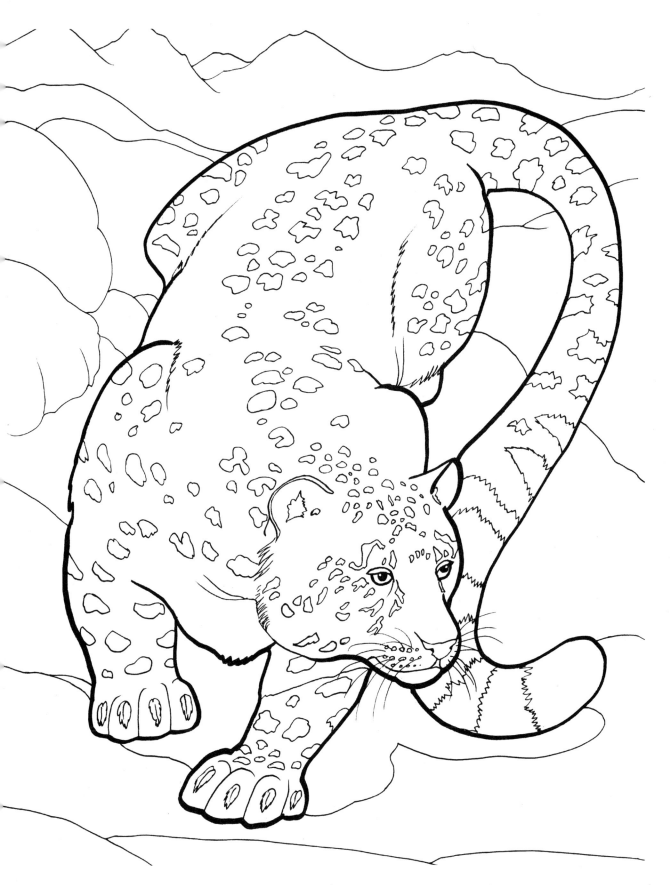

ow Leopard *(Uncia uncia)*. You can find
:se beautiful wild cats high in the mountains
Central Asia. They are shy, solitary creatures
d come out at night. Their coat is wooly and thick, which helps insulate them from the cold. They are able to leap thirty feet into the air to catch prey.

Bactrian Camel *(Camelus bactrianus)*. These two-humped, wild camels live in the deserts of Central and East Asia, where temperatures vary from twenty below zero to over 150 degrees. They are able to survive for weeks without wat[er]. A thirsty camel can drink thirty gallons of wat[er] in less than fifteen minutes!

26

ger *(Panthera tigris)*. These wild cats are the gest land-living carnivores on earth. They ve powerful jaws and canine teeth and can run to forty miles per hour to catch prey. Every tiger's stripes are different, like a human fingerprint. They are native to South and Southeast Asia, China, and Far East Russia.

Malayan Sun Bear *(Helarctos malayanus)*. They are the smallest member of the bear family and are native to the lowland, tropical rainforests of Southeast Asia. Their long tongue allows them to reach into beehives, termite nests, and oth crevices for food. They get their name from t yellow crescent on their chest.

lifornia Condor *(Gymnogyps californianus).*
ese magnificent condors are the largest birds
North America. They have a wingspan of over
nine feet and weigh over eighteen pounds. They
will travel several hundred miles to search for food.
You can find them in south-central California.

29

Przewalski's Horse *(Equus ferus)*. These wild horses were discovered in the late nineteenth century in Central Asia by Russian explorer Nicolai Przewalski. They are short and muscular with pony-like head. They have been bred in captiv and reintroduced into Mongolia.

30